Radical Sports

Skiing

Paul Mason • • • • • • • • • • •

Heinemann Library
Chicago, Illinois

© 2003 Reed Educational & Professional Publishing
Published by Heinemann Library,
an imprint of Reed Educational & Professional Publishing,
Chicago, Illinois

Customer Service 888-454-2279
Visit our website at www.heinemannlibrary.com

Designed by Celia Floyd
Illustrated by Jeff Edwards
Originated by Universal
Printed in Hong Kong

07 06 05 04 03
10 9 8 7 6 5 4 3 2 1

Library of Congress Cataloging-in-Publication Data

Mason, Paul, 1967-
  Skiing / Paul Mason.
      p. cm. -- (Radical sports)
Includes bibliographical references and index.
Summary: Presents an overview of the sport of skiing, including
technique, equipment, guidelines, resources, and safety concerns.
  ISBN 1-58810-628-4 (HC), 1-40340-107-1 (Pbk)
  1. Skis and skiing--Juvenile literature. [1. Skis and skiing.] I.
Title. II. Series.
  GV854.315 .M36 2002
  796.93--dc21
                              2001004805

Acknowledgments

The author and publishers are grateful to the following for permission to reproduce copyright material:
Action plus: 18a; Allsport: 25, 26, 27; Corbis: 24; Images: 29; John Cleare: 18b, 18c; John Noble: 22; Mary Evans
Picture Library: 4, 5; O Robson - Stock Shot: 6, 7a, 7b, 8, 9a, 9b, 9c, 10a, 10b, 11, 12a, 12b, 13a, 13b, 13c, 13d, 14a,
14b, 14c, 15a, 15b, 15c, 16, 17a, 17b, 17c, 17d, 20a, 20b, 21; Skishoot-offshoot: 23.

Cover photograph

Special thanks to Jane Bingham and Steve Buchanan for their comments in the preparation of this book.

Every effort has been made to contact copyright holders of any material reproduced in this book. Any omissions will be
rectified in subsequent printings if notice is given to the publisher.

Some words are shown in bold, **like this.** You can find out what they mean by looking in the
glossary.

CONTENTS

A short history

People have been skiing for over 4000 years! At least that long ago, people in Norway and Sweden were crossing snowy landscapes on long wooden skis. Skiing continued to be just a way of traveling until the mid-nineteenth century when people started to realize that skiing was also a lot of fun!

In the European Alps, people started strapping skis to their feet and sliding down the mountainsides. At about the same time, Norwegian **immigrants** brought skiing to the U.S. People loved the feeling of speed as they raced downhill through the snow.

Another invention was needed before skiing could become really popular—the tow rope. Tow ropes pulled skiers back to the top of the slope without effort. People could learn to ski quickly because it took less time to get to the top of the slope, leaving more time for skiing back down again.

Early skiers didn't have special clothes. Men wore suits and coats, and women wore big skirts.

This photograph from about 1900 shows tourists enjoying a day in the mountains in Switzerland. They are using a rope to help them climb the mountain.

Skiing today

Today there are thousands of ski **resorts** all over the world and many different ways of having fun on the slopes. Skiers can choose downhill skiing, **snowblading,** cross-country, or **telemarking.**

THE SECRET LANGUAGE OF SKIING

These are some of the words skiers use that you might not have heard before:

- **Binding** device that attaches the ski to the ski boot

- **Carving** turning by digging the sides of the ski into the snow, instead of sliding them around

- **Edge** metal edge on the side of the ski that is used to grip the snow during turns

- **Free-heel skiing** skiing across different terrain, including uphill, using skis that attach to the ski boots only at the toe

- **Trail** marked path down the side of a mountain for skiers to follow

- **Snowblading** kind of skiing that uses short skis and a slightly different binding

- **Telemarking** another word for free-heel skiing; the name comes from the Norwegian town of Telemark, where this type of skiing was invented

THE SKIS FOR YOU

Choosing the right skis

The best skis for you depend on your height, weight, and ability level. It's a good idea to rent equipment at first because you get to know the length and style of ski that works best for you. Once you have decided on a particular type, you can invest in your own equipment.

Different words describe the various parts of a ski:

Skiers use poles like these to help them balance during turns and to move across flat ground.

Tail

Edge

Edges cut into the snow and allow the ski to grip during turns.

Tip

Different ski schools give different advice to students about the length of ski they should be using. Some start beginners on very short skis that are easier to control. As they get better, the students move on to longer and longer skis. Other ski schools start beginners on full-length skis.

TOP TIP

On your first ski trip, you will probably rent equipment. Take the advice of the people in the rental shop about what you should be using. If you feel later that different equipment would be better, the shop will let you go back and change your skis or boots.

Traditional skis are great for downhill speed, but not as good for **carving** turns. They have fairly straight edges and are among the longest skis. Telemark skis are for **telemarking,** also called **free-heel skiing.** It combines downhill skiing with cross-country skiing. Telemark skiers can ski up hills as well as down.

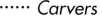

Cross-country skis

These skis are used for skiing along flat ground rather than going downhill and are long and thin for speed.

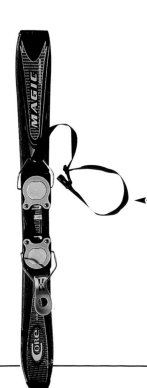

Carvers

Carving skis come in a variety of different lengths. They are shorter than traditional skis and better for carving turns, but don't go as fast in a straight line. The edges of carving skis curve in at the middle, near the boot.

Snowblades

These are shorter than other skis—usually less than three feet (one meter) long. They are easier to control than long skis, and many people find that learning on snowblades is easier than on longer skis, in part because snowbladers don't use poles.

Keep your feet happy!

One of the most important pieces of equipment for skiing is your boots. Uncomfortable boots can make skiing miserable. When your boots cause you pain, it becomes very hard to control your skis, or to think about anything other than how much your feet hurt! If your rented boots start hurting, take them back to the shop and change them for another pair.

CHOOSING BOOTS

Your ski boots need to fit you well without being uncomfortably tight.

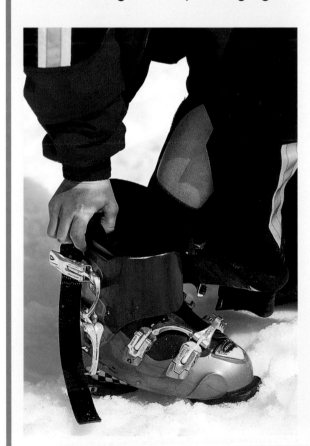

🎿 Stand up in your boots after they're fastened. If your feet feel crushed, you need a larger pair.

🎿 Bend your knees forward so that your shins are resting on the front of the boot. Are they comfortable?

🎿 Lean back so that your calves are against the back of the boot to check for comfort.

🎿 Do the same test leaning from side to side.

🎿 After all this, how do your ankles feel? If they are sore, try another pair of boots.

Bindings

The **binding** is the piece of equipment that attaches the ski to the ski boot. There are different bindings for different types of skis.

Release binding

This binding holds the boot on to the ski at the toe and the heel. As the skier steps into it, it clicks shut. To get your boot out of the binding, you push down with your ski pole on a catch at the side, which releases your heel. In a fall, the binding will snap open. This is to stop the skier's legs from getting badly twisted or broken.

Free-heel binding

This type of binding is used for **telemark** and cross-country skiing. It allows the skier to lift their heel away from the top of the ski. Free-heel bindings release in a fall.

Snowblade binding

This binding is simpler than a release binding. It does not release in a fall, but because snowblades are shorter than other skis, there is less risk of injury.

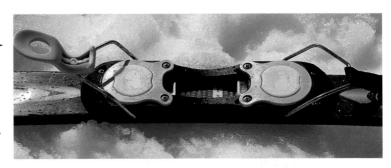

THE RIGHT CLOTHES

It's important to keep warm in the mountains. If you get cold, it becomes harder to concentrate and you will be more likely to have an accident.

Some skiers wear a thick, warm jacket with a single layer of clothes underneath. However, many people prefer to wear several thinner layers of clothes. That way they can add or take away layers according to the temperature.

Helmet ·················▶

This is an essential item. A broken arm or leg will heal, but if you damage your head you may never recover.

Gloves ·················▶

These need to be warm and waterproof. The best ones have a removable lining that allows you to dry the glove out quickly.

SAFETY FIRST

🎿 Always use sunscreen with a high protection factor in the mountains. Your face and lips will burn very quickly without it. This is because sunlight reflects from the snow as well as shines directly on your face.

TOP TIP

🎿 Be prepared for the weather to change very fast. You may have set out on a bright sunny day, but by the afternoon, it could be snowing and windy.

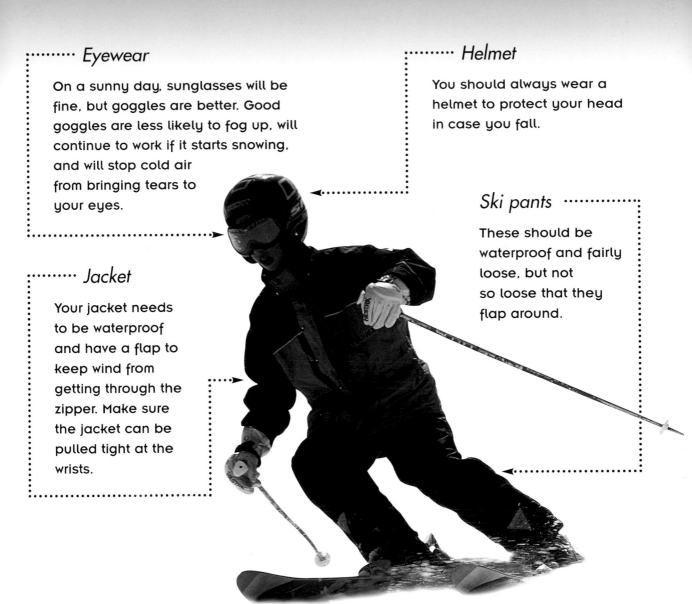

Eyewear

On a sunny day, sunglasses will be fine, but goggles are better. Good goggles are less likely to fog up, will continue to work if it starts snowing, and will stop cold air from bringing tears to your eyes.

Helmet

You should always wear a helmet to protect your head in case you fall.

Ski pants

These should be waterproof and fairly loose, but not so loose that they flap around.

Jacket

Your jacket needs to be waterproof and have a flap to keep wind from getting through the zipper. Make sure the jacket can be pulled tight at the wrists.

It is a good idea to wear a fleece jacket, especially if your outer jacket doesn't have a warm lining. Try to get one that keeps your neck warm when zipped up. Thermal underwear is a layer of clothes, both top and bottom, designed to wear next to your skin. It takes moisture away from your body, stopping the dampness from cooling you down and trapping in heat.

Some skiers wear thin socks, but most prefer special, thick ski socks. A few skiers like them so much that they wear two pairs!

Getting fit

It is worth trying to get into shape before you go on a skiing trip. If you are tired while skiing it becomes hard to learn new techniques. You are also more likely to have an accident.

Warming up

Spend a few minutes stretching your muscles before you ski. This makes it less likely that you will injure a muscle. It also helps you to ski better sooner, since your muscles are already warmed up when you start. When you're finished skiing, do the stretches again. You will find it less painful to leap out of bed the next morning—when you want to go skiing again!

TOP TIP

- As you stretch, breathe deeply from your stomach for six or seven breaths, concentrating on relaxing your muscles. Then stop the stretch.

Calf stretch

Bend one knee while keeping the other leg out straight with your heel on the floor and toe pointing up. You will feel the muscles in your calf and behind your knee stretch. Repeat with the other leg.

Hamstring stretch

Facing a wall, lean in with your hands or forearms flat against it. One leg should be bent and the other straight. Lean in more by bending your elbows; the muscles in the back of your straight leg will stretch. Repeat with the other leg.

Quadricep stretch

Stand with your feet flat on the floor. Lift one foot up behind you and use both hands to pull it in toward your bottom. You will feel your thigh muscle stretch. Make sure you don't arch your back while doing this stretch; your hips should stay parallel with the floor.

Back stretch

Kneel on the floor with your toes pointing backwards. Drop your forehead to the floor with your arms stretched out in front of your head.

Arm stretch

Pull your elbow behind your head with your other hand, so that your arm is dangling down the line of your spine. Repeat with the other arm.

Neck stretch

Lean your head gently to the left, roll it slowly forward and then to the right. Do the same thing in reverse. Never bend your neck backwards: this is bad for it.

Eating for skiing

It is important for skiers to eat enough of the right kind of food. Foods with plenty of **carbohydrates** are good: bread and pasta is ideal. If you eat food with fat in it, like cheese, your stomach takes a long time to break down the fat. Meals with carbohydrates and fat will give you a quick burst of energy from the carbohydrates, then a slow burn of reserve energy from the fat.

THE BASIC SKILLS

The snowplow

Almost all skiers begin by learning a technique called the **snowplow.** The technique gets its name from the shape your skis make, with the tips close together and the **tails** far apart.

The snowplow technique allows you to control the speed of your skis and to choose the direction you turn. It looks very different from more advanced skiing, where the tips and tails of the skis are the same distance apart.

Neutral stance

All skiers, whether they are experts or beginners, should aim to have a **neutral stance.** This means that you should not have more weight on one part of your boots than another. In particular, avoid leaning back on your calves because this will make the skis accelerate away from you.

Slowing down

Push the tails of the skis out using your knees and heels. You will start to slow down.

Stopping

As you push the tails further apart you will come to a stop.

Snowplow turns

Keeping the same amount of weight on each foot will allow you to travel in a straight line. If you think you are going too fast, push the tails of your skis out to slow down. If you are going too slow, bring the tails in a little.

To turn to your right, turn your left hip forward slightly and put extra weight on your left foot.

Your left ski will turn in front of you, bringing the right ski around with it.

SAFETY FIRST

Pick a gentle slope to start skiing! Each ski **resort** has a special area set aside for beginners, called the bunny hills. Classes meet there each morning or afternoon to learn the basics of skiing. These classes are the best way to learn how to ski, with a group of people who are also beginners.

To turn back to the left, repeat the process in reverse, starting by putting extra weight on your right foot.

PARALLEL SKIING

Once you have mastered the **snowplow,** you will want to start skiing with the tips and **tails** of your skis the same distance apart. This is called **parallel skiing.** As with the basic technique, you should try to be in a **neutral stance** most of the time. Your poles will be held loosely under your arms or at your side most of the time, but during turns you might want to use them for balance.

At first, you will only feel comfortable skiing parallel in a straight line across the slope (this is called **traversing)** and your turns will still be done with the snowplow technique. The next step is to make your turns in the parallel position as well. When doing parallel turns, your knees should be bent and your shoulders should be in line with your knees. Try not to twist your body.

Start by crossing the slope to the left with your skis parallel. It is best to start practicing this on a gentle slope. Ease your weight off the **edges** of your skis. You will start to turn down the slope into what is known as the **fall line.** Allow your left ski to move ahead of the right ski. You will speed up slightly. As you begin to move into the fall line, put weight on the **inside edge** of both skis. You will start to turn across the fall line.

 SAFETY FIRST

Be aware of the snow conditions. Remember that it is harder to ski when the snow is frozen and icy.

Continue to put weight on the inside edges of your skis until you have finished your turn.

When you are pointing in the right direction, return to the neutral stance so that you can continue.

To turn to the right, repeat this process in reverse, allowing your left ski to move ahead of your right as you move into the fall line.

The best way to learn advanced techniques is on a gentle hill. Once you feel confident, move on to a slightly steeper one. You will suddenly find the technique harder again, but each time you relearn it on a new hill, it will be easier to master.

ON THE SLOPES

When you get to the **resort** you will need to rent skis and boots if you do not have your own. You will also need to get a lift ticket. This ticket allows you to use the lift system to travel around the mountains. There are three different types of lifts.

Chair lifts

Chair lifts usually carry between two and six people. To catch one, you go through the gate and stand in front of the lift. As you sit down, pull the safety bar down in front of you. Don't forget to push it back up just before getting off!

Cable cars

Cable cars can fit between four and about forty people and you must take off your skis to travel in them. You sit down in smaller ones, but in larger ones you stand up. The small ones are sometimes called "bubbles."

········· Drag lifts

There are two main kinds of drag lifts: button lifts are fitted between your thighs, while T-bars go behind you and are often shared with another skier. Drag lifts have a lot of stretch in them to give you time to get in position before they pull you up the slope. When the light is green, slide slowly through the gate and grab the lift pole. Fit the button or T-bar into position, and wait for the lift to start pulling you up the hill. Lean back a little and relax your legs to stop the lift from pulling you off balance. Drag lifts are rare in the U.S. today.

Trail maps

Trail maps help you to find your way around the resort. They show where the ski runs—called "runs" or "trails"—go, as well as the location of restaurants and first aid posts. The runs are graded using different colors. Trails are given a grade according to how difficult they are to get down. If you are a complete beginner, it is best to stick to the easiest runs at first, while you build up your confidence.

SAFETY FIRST

Drag lifts can sometimes be tricky to use because they can pull quite hard when you first get on. Make sure you are ready to ride the lift. Don't grab the lift pole until you are in position and completely ready. If you take lessons, the instructor will show you how to catch the lifts.

It is important to look after your skiing equipment for two reasons. First, equipment that has not been looked after is much more likely to break. This could cause you to have a nasty accident. Second, skiing equipment that has been cared for works better.

Looking after your skis

The metal **edges** of your skis need to be sharp or you will find it hard to turn. Take a careful look at them to check whether there are any deep scratches on the edges: if there are, you may need to have them sharpened. Take them to a ski shop and have the job done by a professional using a special machine.

The edges of this ski are scratched and blurry, so they need to be sharpened.

It is important to clean wax off the base of a ski.

SAFETY FIRST

Sometimes skiers run over bare ground or rocks, which can gouge a deep chunk out of the bottom of their skis. If this happens, take your skis into the shop as soon as possible. If the gouge has gone through the wax and into the base of the ski, then it will need to be repaired to keep water from soaking in.

The base of your skis will be covered with wax. The wax makes the skis travel faster. As you ski, this wax is slowly worn away, especially if you accidentally go over stones or dirt. Make sure that your skis are waxed regularly— about once for every two to four weeks of use. It is best to have this done by a specialist at a ski shop.

Checking your bindings and boots

Check your **bindings** each morning before you ski by rocking them back and forth and from side to side. If there is any movement, something may need to be tightened up or repaired. You also need to check any buckles on your boots to make sure that nothing has come loose.

The bottom of a ski needs to be waxed regularly.

TOP TIP

Have your skis waxed before you put them away for the summer. This will stop the edges from rusting.

RULES OF THE SLOPES

Collisions between skiers are very dangerous. It is easy to break a leg or an arm, even at slow speeds. Several skiers are killed each year by crashing into one another at high speed. To prevent accidents, there are rules all skiers and snowboarders have to follow.

The downhill skier has the right of way

Skiers further down the slope cannot see you coming from behind them. You must make sure you have plenty of room to pass by. If you do not have room, slow down to their speed until there is plenty of space.

Stick to the marked ski runs

Even if you can see that other skiers have left the ski run, do not follow their tracks. They may be far better skiers than you and able to avoid hazards such as rocks, trees, and **crevasses.** However, they could have skied off a cliff around the corner so it is always best to stick to the marked ski runs.

Safety on the ski run is important. It is best to stick to marked ski runs.

Don't stop in obstructive or invisible positions

The middle of a busy ski run is not the best place to stop for a drink. Neither is just over the top of a hill, where other skiers and snowboarders may not be able to see you until it is too late. Always stop at the edge of the ski run in plain view of downhill skiers.

Keep control of your skis

Runaway skis can do a lot of damage, so make sure they don't slide away as you are putting them on.

Only ride ski runs you can cope with

If you go on a ski run that is too difficult for you, it is far more likely that you will have an accident.

Obey special signs

If a ski run is closed, do not go down it. There may be machinery at work, or the risk of an **avalanche.** You will put yourself, as well as the people who have come to rescue you, in danger.

Always obey warning signs. They are put there to help you avoid danger.

COMPETITIONS

There are several different kinds of skiing competitions and most of them have races for every ability level. Young skiers, inexperienced skiers, skiers with disabilities—these and many others enter competitions of different kinds. To reach the top in any of the events, skiers have to be very talented and extremely fit. Most of the best racers have been skiing since they were three or four years old!

Racers go downhill through a series of gates, which are marked by colored poles that guide the skier down the course. The speed that they can travel is determined by how close together the gates are. Slower races have more gates; faster races have fewer gates.

Slalom
This is the event where the gates are set closest together. Slalom racers have to combine speed with technical skills as they weave their way down the slope.

Giant slalom
Giant slalom is a cross between slalom and downhill. There are more gates than in downhill, but skiers have to make fewer turns than in slalom. There is a variation of giant slalom called super-giant slalom that is more like downhill.

This man is skiing in the giant slalom.

Downhill

This is the fastest and most dangerous of the ski racing events. The gates are there only to guide the skiers along the race route. They ski at speeds that can reach over 60 miles (100 km) per hour. Even so, there are often only fractions of a second between each place.

Ski jumping

In ski jumping competitions, skiers launch themselves from specially built ramps to see who can travel farthest through the air. Some jumpers can cover over 325 feet (100 meters) before landing.

Cross-country

In cross-country events, skiers race around a course to see who can finish in the fastest time. There is also an event called a biathlon that combines cross-country racing with target shooting.

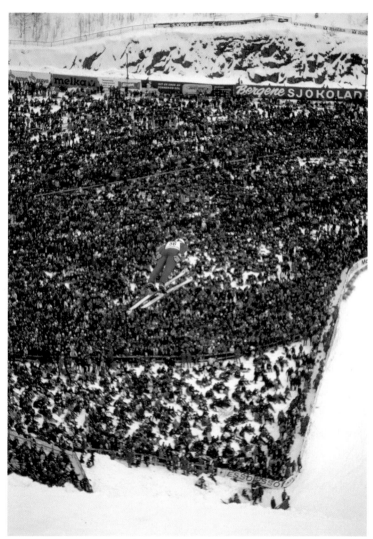

Ski-jumping is one of the most spectacular sports to watch.

SKIING GREATS

The world's top skiers compete in a series of races run by the International Skiing Federation. The most successful racer in each event is crowned World Cup winner at the end of the season. Every four years the skiers get the chance to compete for the ultimate sports prize—an Olympic gold medal.

Every skier on the World Cup Circuit is able to ski extremely fast. Anyone who manages to win even one race has accomplished a tremendous feat. Some skiers, though, stand out by being able to win again and again.

Picabo Street

Picabo Street's father once told Jean-Claude Killy, the French downhill Olympic gold medalist, "I've got a daughter who's going to win an Olympic gold medal some day."

"Good for her," Killy replied, "I hope she does."

In 1998, at the Winter Olympics in Nagano, Japan, Street was returning to competition from a knee injury she had suffered a year before and a serious crash in Sweden ten days previously. She overcame these problems to win the super-giant slalom gold medal, which was presented to her by... Jean-Claude Killy!

Picabo Street celebrates her gold medal at the 1998 Winter Olympics.

The Herminator—Hermann Maier—
shows his powerful technique during
a giant slalom race.

"The Herminator"

Hermann Maier, also known as "The
Herminator" because of his aggressive
skiing style, is one of the most successful
skiers today. Maier joined the Austrian
youth team at the age of fifteen, but was
soon dropped because he was too small.
He took a job as a bricklayer's apprentice,
and seven years later the Herminator was
big enough to force his way back into the
Austrian team. He went on to win an
Olympic gold medal at the 1998 Nagano
Games.

Franz Klammer

Franz Klammer won 23 World Cup downhill
races in his career. In 1976 he was in one of
the most exciting events ever at the Winter
Olympics in Innsbruck, Austria. Klammer
was behind coming into the final stretch of
the course, but he skied the rest of the
course thrillingly, always seeming as
though he was about to crash. He just
managed to sneak ahead to claim first
place and the gold medal.

Annemarie Moser-Proll

Annemarie Moser-Proll is another legendary
Austrian skier, who learned to ski at four
years old and won the women's World Cup
a record six times. In 1973, she won eleven
downhill races in a row. She also won a
gold medal in 1980 at the Winter Olympics.

ENDLESS WINTER

It is always winter somewhere around the world. It may be bright and sunny in the Rocky Mountains in June and July, but at the same moment it is cold and snowy in the South American Andes. There is always somewhere you can go skiing.

Some people love skiing so much that they follow the snow around the world. In March they may be working in a **resort** in Colorado or the European Alps. By July or August they could be in New Zealand or Argentina. Whatever type of job that comes up is fine— ski instructor, lift attendant, or dishwasher in a restaurant—as long as it leaves time for skiing.

Skiers enjoy the skiing as well as the scenery at Mount Whitcombe in New Zealand.

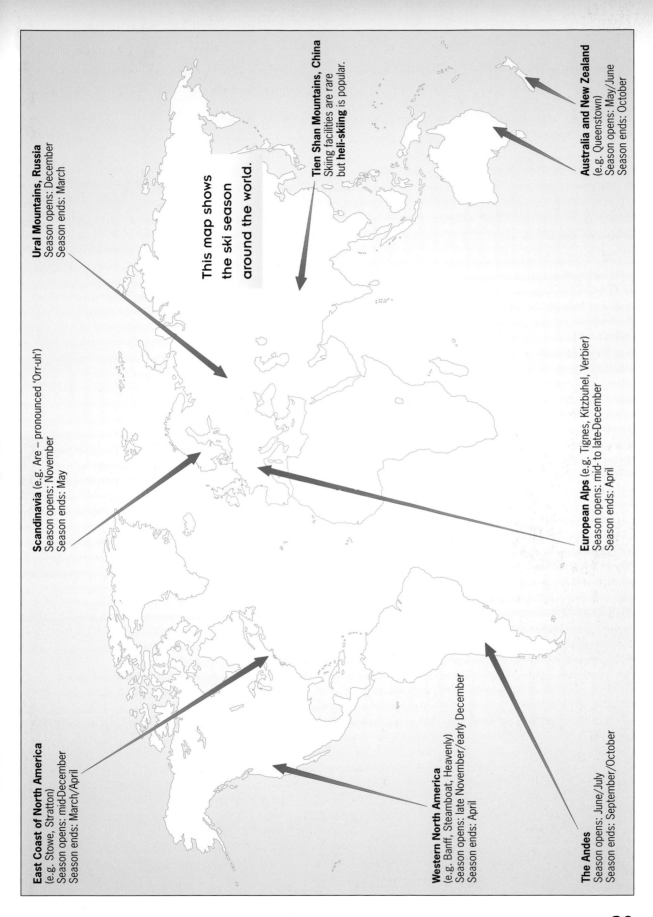

Ural Mountains, Russia
Season opens: December
Season ends: March

This map shows
the ski season
around the world.

Tien Shan Mountains, China
Skiing facilities are rare
but **heli-skiing** is popular.

Australia and New Zealand
(e.g. Queenstown)
Season opens: May/June
Season ends: October

Scandinavia (e.g. Åre – pronounced 'Orr-uh')
Season opens: November
Season ends: May

European Alps (e.g. Tignes, Kitzbühel, Verbier)
Season opens: mid- to late-December
Season ends: April

East Coast of North America
(e.g. Stowe, Stratton)
Season opens: mid-December
Season ends: March/April

Western North America
(e.g. Banff, Steamboat, Heavenly)
Season opens: late November/early December
Season ends: April

The Andes
Season opens: June/July
Season ends: September/October

GLOSSARY

avalanche   sudden movement of snow down a mountainside

binding   device that attaches your ski boot to your ski

carbohydrate   food that the body uses for energy

carving   digging the edges of your skis into the snow so they don't slip sideways; when you look back up the hill, a carved turn has left an obvious line showing the path you took

crevasses   deep cracks in ice or rocks

edge   metal strip that runs down each side of a ski; the edges allow skis to grip the snow during turns

fall line   direction that a rock would travel if you rolled it down a slope (usually straight downhill)

free-heel skiing   another word for telemarking

heli-skiing   type of skiing where skiers are dropped off at the top of an empty slope by helicopter

hypothermia   condition of having an unusually low body temperature; although people can recover from mild hypothermia, it is possible to die from severe hypothermia

immigrants   people who come from somewhere else to live in a new country

inside edge   edge of the ski that points toward the top of the slope or the inside of a turn

neutral stance   basic position for all skiers, in which you stand evenly on your skis without putting extra weight on any part of your boots or skis

parallel skiing   technique where you ski with the tips and tails of your skis an equal distance apart

resort   place where people come to ski, that will have lifts, restaurants, and other facilities for skiers

snowblading   kind of skiing that uses very short skis and no poles

snowplow   position that most people use to learn to ski; with the tips of the skis close together and the tails of the skis further apart

tail   back part of the ski

telemarking   type of skiing using a binding that attaches the ski to the boot only at the toe

trail   marked route down the mountain for skiers; also called a run

traversing   skiing across a slope instead of down it

USEFUL ADDRESSES

Canadian Ski and Snowboard
Association
18 Central Avenue
Ottawa, Ontario
CANADA

U.S. Ski and Snowboard Association
P.O. Box 100
1500 Kearns Blvd.
Park City, UT 84060

International Ski Federation
Marc Hodler House
Blochstrasse 2
CH-3653 Oberhofen/Thunersee
SWITZERLAND

MORE BOOKS TO READ

Fraser, Andy. *Snowboarding.* Chicago: Heinemann Library, 1999.

Maurer, Tracy. *Snow Skiing.* Vero Beach, Fla.: Rourke Publishing, 2001.

Stiefer, Sandy. *Marathon Skiing.* New York: Rosen Publishing Group, 2001.

U.S. Olympic Skiing Committee. *A Basic Guide to Skiing and Snowboarding.* Milwaukee: Gareth Stevens, 2002.

INDEX